Other titles in the UWAP Poetry series (established 2016)

Our Lady of the Fence Post by J. H. Crone

Border Security by Bruce Dawe

Melbourne Journal by Alan Loney

Star Struck by David McCooey

Dark Convicts by Judy Johnson

Rallying by Quinn Eades

Flute of Milk by Susan Fealy

A Personal History of Vision by Luke Fischer

Snake Like Charms by Amanda Joy

Charlie Twirl by Alan Gould

Afloat in Light by David Adès

Communists Like Us by John Falzon

Hush by Dominique Hecq

Preparations for Departure by Nathanael O'Reilly

The Tiny Museums by Carolyn Abbs

The Criminal Re-Register by Ross Gibson

Fingertip of the Tongue by Sarah Rice

Chromatic

Paul Munden

Paul Munden's poetry first appeared in Faber's *Poetry Introduction 7*. A Gregory Award winner, he has published four collections: *Henderskelfe* (Talking Shop, 1989), with photographs of Castle Howard by Peter Heaton; *Asterisk* (Smith|Doorstop, 2011), based on Shandy Hall, former home of Laurence Sterne; *Analogue/Digital, New & Selected Poems* (Smith|Doorstop, 2015); and *The Bulmer Murder* (Recent Work Press, 2017). He is a Postdoctoral Research Fellow at the University of Canberra, where he is also Program Manager for the International Poetry Studies Institute (IPSI), running the annual Poetry on the Move festival. He is Associate Editor of *Axon: Creative Explorations*, and the literary journal, *Meniscus*. He was reader for Stanley Kubrick from 1988-98, and has been Director of the UK's National Association of Writers in Education (NAWE) since 1994. He has worked as conference poet for the British Council and edited *Feeling the Pressure: Poetry and science of climate change* (British Council, 2008). He has lived in Bulmer, North Yorkshire, for over 30 years, now dividing his time between Yorkshire and Canberra.

Paul Munden
Chromatic

First published in 2017 by
UWA Publishing
Crawley, Western Australia 6009
www.uwap.uwa.edu.au

UWAP is an imprint of UWA Publishing
a division of The University of Western Australia

This book is copyright. Apart from any fair dealing
for the purpose of private study, research, criticism
or review, as permitted under the *Copyright Act 1968*,
no part may be reproduced by any process without
written permission.
Enquiries should be made to the publisher.

Copyright © Paul Munden 2017
The moral right of the author has been asserted.

National Library of Australia
Cataloguing-in-Publication entry:
Munden, Paul, author.
Chromatic / Paul Munden.
ISBN: 9781742589534 (paperback)
English poetry—21st century.
Australian poetry—21st century.

Designed by Becky Chilcott, Chil3
Typeset in Lyon Text by Lasertype
Printed by Lightning Source

This project has been assisted by the Australian
Government through the Australia Council, its arts
funding and advisory body.

 uwapublishing

Acknowledgements

Poems have previously appeared in the following publications and exhibitions:

Journals and newspapers:
The Canberra Times; Cordite; Mascara; OC Magazine; Rabbit; Stride; UnderBridge Poetry; Uneven Floor; Westerly

Anthologies:
Festschrift for Katherine Gallagher (Circle Time Press, 2015)
Seam: Prose Poetry Project (IPSI, 2015)
Pulse: Prose Poems (Recent Work Press, 2016)
Tract: Prose Poems (Recent Work Press, 2017)

'Modulations to a Minor Key' was shortlisted for the *Aesthetica* Creative Writing Award 2016 and published in the associated anthology.

Exhibitions:
Traces and Hauntings (Belconnen Arts Centre, 2015)
The Encyclopædia of Forgotten Things (Belconnen Arts Centre, 2016)
Beauties and Beasts (Belconnen Arts Centre, 2017)
Bill Poetries ('Noted' Festival, Canberra, 2017)

The 'Keys' and 'Fire' poems were first published within chapbooks under the Authorised Theft imprint.

A selection of these poems was published as *The Bulmer Murder* (Recent Work Press, 2017)

I should like to thank my colleagues at the University of Canberra for all their encouragement, creative and critical help, also those in the wider poetry community who made me so welcome, so quickly, in Australia. Special thanks go to Terri-ann White for her commitment to this book, also to my family, who so strongly supported the Australian venture that brought the work about. A number of individuals are acknowledged by initials below the poem titles; others will recognise their invaluable influence in particular poems, however obliquely they may be referenced.

Contents

PART 1
Toccata **12**
I stared **14**
Trench Cello **15**
From *The Encyclopædia of Forgotten Things* **17**
Fugue **20**
A Diagram **28**
Chopinesque **29**
A Night at the Opera **30**
Kick/Recall **33**
Spiders **34**
Modulations (to a major key) **36**
Modulations (to a minor key) **39**
Foxed **42**
Keys **45**
Rat Tales **47**
A Speckled Hen **55**
Country Gardens **56**
Brideshead Revisited **58**
Prototype **59**
Miss Willmott's Ghost **60**
Molehills **62**
Ladybirds **64**
English Pastoral **65**
Christmas Diptych **66**

PART 2
La Tempesta **70**
Venetian Lullaby **76**
Transpositions **77**
And when— **80**
Here and There **81**
Carnarvon Gorge **82**
Four Seasons in One Day **83**
One midsummer night **84**
Sightings **85**
Turtles **90**
The Shallows **91**
Heron Island **92**
Twice now the outward adventure **96**
How could he have known— **97**
An act of love **98**

Touch **100**
His deceptive memory **101**
Ply **102**
To think— **105**
Page 147 **106**
The King Lear Catalogue,
1976-2015 **107**
Muldoonery **108**

PART 3
Tethered **112**
Fire **113**
Alphabet Jigsaw **115**
Bring Me the Head **116**
Camille **118**
Meringue **119**
Country House Visitor, Yorkshire,
c. 1996 **120**
Macbeth **121**
Fair Bianca **123**
Midsummer, Brownsea, 1965 **124**
Freckle **125**

The Weathercock **127**
The Larder **128**
See— **130**
In the Capuchin catacomb **131**
Chromatic **132**
A Footnote **135**
Four Poster **136**
Fractures **137**
redruM **138**
Steadicam **139**
All Work and No Play **140**
The Bulmer Murder **141**
For Sale: Number 453 **156**
1768 **157**
The Pub with No Beer **158**
The Soldier's Tale **160**
In a Country Churchyard **162**

Notes **164**

PART 1

His fingers had the noses of weasels
　　　　　—Sylvia Plath, 'Little Fugue'

Toccata

It starts again, the screeching
early morning practice,
raucous skills brought out
of semi-retirement,
cleaving the rural calm
as if this is all it's good for
now, a training base for war.

       Maybe you remember it
       from the time your pram
       rocked on its springs
       and your growing wail
       was the echo of a siren.
       You sense the out-of-nowhere
       wall of colossal sound

and throw yourself to ground
with something close
to justification,
the Tornado
cutting through the air
above you as it hugs
the contours of the land—

   cornfields rippling
   in its wake—and sucks
   the breath from hill and dale,
   leaving the garden drained
   of colour, like a face in shock,
   the world in camouflage:
   re-audible birdsong

so petite;
pastoral light
frail as my father's bones
beneath the hospital sheet;
his voice—mere whisperings
of hard-won reportage...
Butcher Island...

   Yes?... nothing more.
   A bewildered accomplice,
   I scour the map
   for what, if anything, remains
   and marvel at how you pick
   your small self up
   from your own shadow.

I stared

at Uncle Ern's bald head,
his huge ears, listening
to his tearful testament,
which was simply a word-
for-word account

*that no such undertaking
has been received, and that
consequently this country
is at war with Germany.*

Trench Cello

No Stradivari, this, no Amati, and no
voluptuous Cremonese curves
echoing your darling—

but still you handle it with care, heavy-duty
foursquare English oak, standard issue,
or so it looks until

you open its front to reveal ammunition
of a different sort, everything
you need to kill despair

or whatever dark, life-diminishing moments
take control of you and your comrades
biding your time in mud.

You unpack it like any other kit, its coiled
metal strings, ebony fingerboard
and tailpiece, bridge and spike—

all assembled as fast as a rifle, soundpost
in place like the prop of a dugout.
You tighten the bow, blow

across the special little hollow at the end
like the top of a bottle of stout
for an A to tune it—

or you did. Because *this* was *then* and the desire
has now deserted you. All you want
is to be rid of it—

let someone else learn this historical drill, bring
back the thin, muddied sound in all its
charm, and call it *plaintive*.

From *The Encyclopædia of Forgotten Things*

When you hurl the paratrooper from your bedroom window, he hangs for a moment against the sun, making you screw up your eyes. His plastic backpack flips open, the red-white-blue silk billows in the air, and our childhoods linger, conscripted into a slow, slow freefall that matters so much we hold our synchronised breaths... until the crash on gravel—the disjointed figure lying in the yard, staring at the sky— and a silence in which we each expect the other to make some move to retrieve, to try again.

*

Every week, she has trudged the quarter mile to church, taken up her solitary bench, opened the hymn book, and done her best. But every week there is a new fluffed note or erroneous chord that adds to the catalogue of mistakes forgotten by everyone—except her. And today the archival muscle of her fingers has reached its limit. In the shuffling silence as the congregation prepares to draw breath, there's a cracking of joints, and an inexplicable click of her teeth like a malfunctioning machine, followed by nothing.

*

Years after the old stone farmhouse had been sold, and yet another attic was being cleared, there it was, the plywood replica he had crafted in such detail: two staircases, blue patterned wallpaper, and pale gold carpet, an offcut of the real. There were simplifications, of course. The stovepipe in the living room was matt black dowel, but angled in precise correlation to the one that channelled smoke around the high window: that—like all the others—was a square-cut hole, enabling the children to look in at the world they already inhabited. Their small hands could reach through to lay breakfast, and move the chairs for extra guests. The roof hinged back so their bedrooms were a free-for-all. Only one room was harder to explore, and so they missed the arguments, the toll taken by the hours the encyclopædic venture had incurred. He blew, and watched clumps of dust drifting through memory's build. He could still feel the rasp of the saw through the ply, still smell the paint taking so long to dry as Christmas morning came around.

*

Raw silk, calico, sleeveless cotton in burgundy or cerise, a timeless blue skirt... Her stage wardrobe is arranged with an algorithm calculated to make you forget. Stripes and checks in black and white, white and black (or is it navy?)... Each day she appears as if fresh from the shops, charms you with the illusion of the new. The weather is glossed with the same, skilful repetition of the unique: every cloud a sweet nothing, every sunburst bright as your breakfast juice, every snowflake an unpredictable kiss.

*

The soloist walks to the front of stage for Brandenburg #4, and the audience applauds. He grips the violin and its small maroon cushion between collarbone and chin, and as the welcome subsides in a predictable arc there are two or three unnerving seconds where other, long-gone instruments are in his grasp: the oboe so grimed with school-bag dirt he immersed it in the bath; and the cello in its soft case slung over his shoulder as he cycled home, the spike slipping free and catching in the wheel arch of a passing car. The noise of it splinters from the dwindling applause. The last few hand-claps are the damp patterings of the oboe's ruined felts. Then silence, composure, the chosen gleam of varnished spruce and maple ribs, horsehair stretched on carbon fibre delicately balanced between fingers and thumb, ready to erase.

Fugue
i.m. Clement McWilliam, 1934-2007

#1

You take your place
hidden at the console
high above the quire.
There's a mirror, angled
to give you a view
of the conductor below—
his balding head
and outstretched arm.
You know exactly how
to pre-empt the drop
of his hand, to gauge
the time-lag

in the heave of air
from when your fingers
depress the keys—a heave
that was once the work
of seventy men—until
it forces through the pipes
and turns to music,
music rising to the vaults
then circling the nave
so that stone and glass
add reverberating voice
to the simple hymn.

Once, I followed you
up the narrow spiral
staircase into the loft,
waited in the shadows
for the hush that fell
after the final verse,
then the blessing,
and watched you begin
the astonishing reprise
while casual worshippers
drifted from their pews,
wondering why others

looked set to stay.
But then they heard it—
that same melodic line
we had all just sung,
turning at your touch
to an improvised fugue,
the one familiar phrase
building in the air
like a cathedral
hanging in a cathedral,
its colossal complexity
beggaring belief.

I watched the ease
with which you pulled
and pushed the stops
without your hands
ever leaving the multiple
manuals, or so it seemed,
such was the speed
and physical grace
of your thought,
the precision of each
new generative whim
and its intricate

locking to the next.
Your feet worked out
a parallel, nimble dance,
pivoting between heel
and toe, grounding
the ephemeral
Trumpet and Tremulant
with growling tones
of Bourdon, Bombarde
and Double Open Wood.
The instant your casual
masterpiece emerged

it was gone. Is that true?
Or does the fragment
of an echo still linger
high in the vaults,
a memory inaudible
to the human ear
but still rippling
through human lives
as they make their way
over the river, heading
for home, or other long
dark evenings ahead?

#2 *(repeat ad infinitum)*

and once again, evensong's muted tones
give way to the lurid lights of the pub

where you take your place at the machine,
your organist's fingers itching for more—

strawberry | lemon | lemon | plum | lime

and so it begins, the nudge and swing,
the relentless attempt to match

the spooling mathematics in your head
with the clunking fall of coloured fruits—

orange | lemon | cherry | cherry | lime

in that elusive cadence. You hold—with
never-diminishing reserves of hope

while the coins from your pocket drop
into the hungry mechanical abyss

plum | plum | plum | plum | *banana*

—the same old skin on which you slip
each night before *time gentlemen* is called,

but as you make your penniless way
back home the variations still play out—

cherry | strawberry | melon | lemon | lime

in search of the satisfying crash of coins
in the hopper—the one that never stops—

#3

An endless summer. Exams all done.
An invisible future hung in the heat.
With time on my hands, I mapped
a six-lane track onto the field
between the Bishop's Palace
and Wolvesey Castle's ruined walls,
marked it on paper and transferred it
to grass with pegs and string, then
wheeled the trolley's dribbling
chalk and limestone mix
along each straight and around each
bend, before crouching to a start
and finally letting the race in my head
move into the muscles of my legs.

On other days, as clockless weeks
stretched out like sunshine,
I would sit inside and draw
scrolled clefs on the open staves,
listening while you, master of fugue,
explained its theory.
My own slow counterpoints
crawled soundlessly onto the page,
a soft, graphite slide or scuff
on fibrous paper, coaxed
by your patience and your pleasure

at seeing music take shape
from the simplest of ideas.
And still they crawl.

A Diagram

Lines of scuffed chalk
on playground brick.
The wicket-keeper is practising
piano, yards behind the wall,
but as another tennis ball

loops through the air,
the small batsman must stare
into the sun, believing
the bails behind him might fall.

Chopinesque

So small, the cast metal hand
in the glass case, no match
for the phenomenal stretch
of notes in the manuscript.
I shadow it with my own—

imagine how your fingers kept
faith with your musical mind,
turning the tendons' strain
into astonishing arabesque.

A Night at the Opera

He can't take his eyes off her—
her sumptuous blue velvet dress,
the movement of her cleavage
as she breathes, her hair a gold
embodiment of theatrical light—

but when she raises her hand
from her lap it's to proffer
the intimacy of her gaze
not to him but the shenanigans
in the dolls' house onstage.

*

It was the Age of Innocence.
They sat in the comfortable dark,
watching 1920s New York
through the lens of '93, Gounod
via Scorsese giving Faust

an Italianate French twist.
The moment La Pfeiffer
turned to camera—her face
filling the screen—they knew a lover
had forever driven a wedge

between them, and when the final
Cappa/De Fina credits rolled,
they sat in catatonic silence
acknowledging the unspeakable:
the pact with the devil you know.

*

Reprise, lentement, a l'infini
||: With each languid repeat
of her gesture he sees
more clearly the perfect world
in which he plays no part:

how her husband buys her
opera glasses every week
as another might buy flowers
da capo al fine :|| gilded white,
lacquered, pearlescent pink,

or the colour of the night,
glimmering with stars.
He feels his being has shrunk
to a failing heartbeat unsure
of its purpose. He stares

at the miniature cinemascope
window, the ticker-tape
seatback crawl of language
in all its emotional plea,
translated by digitised rote.

Kick/Recall

Putting it to wash, he finds his old maroon t-shirt still holds the ghost of sticky white tape that fixed the electrode to his chest, a fibrous square with a penny-sized absence at its centre somehow meshed to the cotton, even after all these years. He closes the door and watches the machine kick suddenly into reverse—as does the ambulance, taking him back from city hospital to rural dark, its blue light outblinking the sleepy village. He's slumped at his desk, mumbling answers to questions, questions, watching the empty bottle reacquire its pale orange allure, and feeling the strange jerk of his body twisting the child-proof cap of the plastic container into place. Then there's another kick, a further reverse of the machine, back into the future, saving him from himself.

Spiders

You remove my glasses,
easing the pain in the bridge
of my nose where the metal
frame has cut through skin
and left a rusty line.
'Is that a *stitch*?'
The bulbous machine

>glides towards me
>and I rest my unshaven chin
>on a bed of tissues.
>You sit to one side and shine
>a pencil-thin torch-
>beam into the small
>black hole

to strike up
black forked lightning—a map
of veins like crazed pottery,
cartoon trees...
'Fighting spiders,' you say
before you fire
a puff of air

       straight at my eye,
       testing for glaucoma.
       It makes me cry.
       With one hand you stretch
       my eyelids apart,
       leaving me no option
       but to watch

your fingertip closing in,
placing the transparent petal
in the drift of my tears
with such intimate touch,
turning it until it
settles and my vision
clears.

       'Which is brightest,
       the red or the green?'
       'They look… to be honest
       I haven't had much sleep.'
       You slide and pluck the lens away
       between finger and thumb.
       'Now, you try.'

Modulations (to a major key)

#1

When the forceps had done their worst
and the doctor went to hose off his boots

it was the midwife's turn, her gentle art
a practised remedy for the brutish birth.

She sat through the night, massaging
the baby's head back into shape,

her thumbs' soft pressure bringing
patience, care, hope and skill to bear

on the still elastic skull, while the mother,
exhausted beyond belief, slept on

until morning, to find her maimed son
the very vision of perfection.

#2

Each Monday evening, the sheer routine
would weigh him down. He felt sick

just packing his trunks and towel,
heading for the freezing chlorinated pool

where he clutched the polystyrene tablet
shaped like a tombstone and got

nowhere. How he ached seeing his own
daughter struggle in the same way,

the inflatable arm-bands somehow
failing to keep her afloat—until the day

she forgot them, and never noticed,
buoyed up by self-confidence alone.

#3

Her mother lifts the dress from the box
where it's been cosseted for thirty years

as if from a bed of ash, aghast
at how the antique lace has discoloured,

but she hangs it to bleach
in the encouraging sun, then gently

immerses it in a bath of cold water,
watching the offensive tan seep out

as if from a tea bag, but still not enough,
so then the unthinkable—entrusting it

to a machine, like shifting a pop song
up one semitone for the triumphal chorus.

Modulations (to a minor key)

#1

We check out, ready for the long haul
home, with a couple of hours to spare.

We head for a final swim, picking our way
around toppled palm trees, strewn

on the sand by last night's storm
like giant cocktail sticks at a party.

It's hot again; we're filmed with sweat
and offered a random room

in which to shower, but find the bed
occupied by the thin polythene ghost

of the bridegroom we saw wandering
along the shore in his immaculate suit.

#2

An unassuming cardboard box
is retrieved from the attic. She opens it

and layers of tissue paper breathe
like petticoats as her hands delve

towards the antique Irish lace
that's been wrapped away twice now,

but this time, for all her mother's care,
it's a disaster. It's as if the dress

has been hauled from a peat bog,
stained with tannin, and her wish

to take new ownership is matched
by a momentous fear that she must.

#3

He re-enters the small Saxon church
and chooses an empty pew at the back.

He's come to see the flowers once more
before they fade—aware

that alongside other parishioners
his presence is somehow a fraud

but the sight and scent of the white lilies
is to him a sacrament, revealing

the mystery of time: how the past
presses towards him even as the future

recedes—all those new people here
assembling; people he'll never know.

Foxed

1

When he stumbles on the slack wet shape
in the long grass, like something stillborn,
he knows it's his neighbour
who's chucked it there to rot. It's war

that he'll try to refuse as he steps around
the greasy corpse and eyes up
boughs of berried holly within reach
of his shears, sticking to his task.

The last time he walked through the field
the grass was cropped short, bleached
from where the wedding tent had stood.
There were straw bales, still casually placed

for guests long gone, the odd empty bottle
of Black Sheep, and a trail of Love Hearts.

2

He opens the door of the dark compactum
in the bedroom of his childhood home.
Inside, there's a mirror, spotted with rust:
whichever way he looks, his face is fifty years

adrift. There are drawers for shirts, socks,
handkerchiefs, and a tie rack that folds up
flat against the door. He can't see to the back
of the topmost shelf but can feel—

before he reaches it—the small, hard ball
of the nose and the smooth haired
contours of the head. And as he pulls it
from its den, the soft flared brush falls

loose. He wraps it around his shoulders;
fastens the bakelite clasp beneath the jaw.

3

He can taste the fizz of sherbet, still catch
occasional words, looped by purple-pink,
and put a face to every kiss-chased name,
but he remembers, too, how no-one

would believe him when he ran in,
breathless, telling his own tale of Mr Tod,
or rather, the hairless cubs he had raced
the wooded length of the drive, at dusk.

Hairless—there was the rub. But he told it
like it was, and even now will not revise
his apparent hallucination as he picks
loose blood-red berries from the basket,

sits by the fire and opens a book, noticing
how the pages match his liver-spotted hands.

Keys

Clear blue Yorkshire sky. Church done. Potatoes in their goose fat crisping to perfection—you can smell them as the gravel to the front porch crunches underfoot. You wave to the last villager as you turn the key and feel it break: a perforated coin between finger and thumb, useless money, the jagged rest-of-it barrelled in the door. The slow dagger of an icicle drips on your head. You rummage in the shed, searching for the thinnest of thin-nosed pliers, your thoughts already turning to broken glass.

*

All around the keyhole, scratches on the brass, and deeper gouges into the surrounding wood, as if the world's worst drunk had made it this far from the Cock and Bull, then lost it big time, howling at the moon. The house is silent as he walks from the flagstoned hallway to the kitchen. He knows what he'll find as he lifts the lid of a massive earthenware jar by the sink. A spare sackful, riddled with weevils, clutters the pantry. He remembers the last outing, thirsty as hell, pulling the lead that now hangs like a streak of blood on the wall.

*

Stripped to your boxers, you try to straighten up and take it on the chin. Why *do* skeletons grin? This one wears a trilby, might as well be smoking a cigar. You watch the articulating bones, sense the response in your own slack spine. The clavicle turns as the doctor lifts one lifeless arm, his voice fading to a whispering drone, and what you overhear, instead, is the time the locum picked up the phone for another opinion—about *a man in his fifties*... You looked around, finding no one else in the room.

*

Equally strange are the old locks, dismembered, in a dusty basket. Excavated mortices: brass casings, levers, springs. Meaningless pieces, their memories shot. The neighbouring jars hold nails, screws, nuts *and* bolts—a rusting semblance of utility. Autumn sunlight slants through cobwebs in the late afternoon, a gentle inquisition. Will anything muster the minimal gleam for a further reprieve? Nothing stirs. Somehow the rumourous groans of misfit futures have been heard—scrapings and squealings that make this silent bedlam a preferable home.

*

He perfected the habit, ducking his head under the keystoned arch. Took pleasure finding everything in its place, blowing dust from the label of just the right wine. He knew the number of apples—each wrapped in newspaper—remaining in the racks. So today, when he grazed his balding scalp, and wiping it, found a smear of blood and lichen on his hand, he shouldn't have been surprised at the paper husks. The empty tray of warfarin. The droppings. The dry roast pork. His wife taking off in a huff.

Rat Tales
(for LW)

Smell a rat,
see a rat,
kill a rat...
Rats is life!

   *

A musty smell
lingered
in the air
above the bed.

She stripped
the bedding,
emptied
every drawer,

the wardrobe,
scrubbed every
square inch
of the room

to no effect
and when
she began to peel
the wallpaper

knew that she
had started
to shred
her own mind.

She perched
a ladder
on the landing
to gain access

to the loft,
then lost
her nerve—
summoned

her neighbour
who lifted
the hatch
and shone light

over the pale
yellow lagging
laid between
joists, noted

how the air
was doubly
foul and called
for a shovel.

He lifted strip
after strip,
knowing
what he'd find—

how the body
would look
so much bigger
than imagined

and still haired
as if alive,
so that when
he slid the steel

under its bulk
he half expected
it to writhe
and run at him...

But he held
to his task,
backed his way
down the steps

and dropped
the carcass
on a bonfire
in the garden.

The next day
he returned
to the heap
of warm ash

and saw it:
the perfect skull,
baked white
within the grey.

He knelt, stared
into the space
that was an eye,
and all it took

was the gentlest
tap of his nail
for the collapse
into pure dust.

    *

I used to sleep
in the attic
with his baby
and watch

red squirrels
in the oak tree
by the window.
One morning

before I woke
he rushed in
screaming
and I grabbed

the child mere
seconds before
a fat rat ran
around the rim

of the cot, then
onto the bed
and disappeared
under the pillow

where I still
pictured my head
as he battered it
with his spade

again and again
until the shrieks
subsided (and
who knew whose).

    *

He took a stroll
round the garden
before turning in,
listening out

for the familiar
owl's soft call
when something
caught his eye—

a luminous cloud
pulsating above
the compost heap,
and as he walked

towards it
the vision seethed
and atomised
into a swarm

of moonlit rats,
robed in white
as if escaped
from an asylum,

and like one, they
turned on him,
fearless,
and he ran.

    *

Years later
you still hear
the rusty creak
of the old door

as it opened
onto the smell
of musty corn;
still see—there,

through grainy
half-light
in the corner
of the barn,

from floor
to rafters—
a heavy chain
of rats, nose

to tail, as if
climbing
the twisted rope
of themselves.

   *

And they are all
descended from
Mr and Mrs
Samuel Whiskers,

children and great
grandchildren—
there is no
end to them.

A Speckled Hen

When Rosalind, Countess of Carlisle
discovered temperance,
the Castle's supply of Audit Ale
was poured down the drains,

though for every story of every bottle
of finest claret dumped in the lake,
another gives them to a hospital,
or reckons that no dipsomaniac

would have touched them, the wine
so foul, the corks like fungus,
with Rosalind—a speckled hen—
still flitting among us

like a ghost, refusing to elucidate:
I go barefoot, barefoot, barefoot!

Country Gardens

Percy Grainger,
               no stranger
                           to the Proms, has managed to arrange a
Last Night
        performance, though he's nowhere in sight,
                                17 September 1988,
some 27 years
        after his death. The audience fears
                                the worst but hears
the wooden robot
        punch the Steinway's first pure note
                                    only half a beat late
and intrigue
        sets in as it makes a pretty good fist of the Grieg

                *

but a plastic flower?
        Standards any lower
                would make Percy Thrower
turn in his grave.
        The BBC sound archive
                                still holds the live
recording of when his puff
        of pipe-smoke was enough
                                for a pig to cough
on cue for *The Archers*.
        His later departures
                show how knowledge is

oh so transferable:
                      for BBC read ICI; commercialism preferable

                *

and what comes wafting across the lawn
                            as the sun
                                    goes down
on England
      is the Jools Holland Band
                        on its Forest tour, circa two-thousand,
a brassy remix
              of timeless classics
                                giving us our fix
of the dead
          but not gone. In the central bed
                                a deep red hybrid
musk rose thrives
            on the mulched decomposition of other lives.

Brideshead Revisited

I stand where Jeremy Irons
would smoke a cigarette,
my poems acting as captions
for photographs of the estate.
A tourist asks me how I cope

with Lord Sebastian in a mope
or drunk and I tell him a twisted
version of the truth—
something to be going along with.

Prototype

He discovers the slim pack
of perforated grey plastic
cards in their original wallet,
remembers how the slot
in the wall would tease

one gently from his grip
in exchange for twenty crisp
pound notes, and by magic
return it to his address.

Miss Willmott's Ghost

So rich, so young—
you thought almost nothing
of that birthday cheque
on your breakfast plate,
a fairy godmother seeding
a lifetime's obsession;
money's oblique

>   translation into beauty
>   and eventually, debt;
>   the girl turned spinster.
>   Were you losing your wits
>   when you cast the magic dust
>   from your pockets—
>   *Eryngium Giganteum*—

in every garden you visited?
Silvery blue thistles
with spiky ruffs stood
like devilish choristers
doing what they must
and with such structural grace
that no one had the heart

        to pull them out,
        the eponymous nickname
        taking hold in every border
        of England—sea-holly scattered
        so far from the sea—
        while your own patch suffered
        a financial drought.

You planted a daffodil field
with trip wires, patrolled
the booby-trapped territory
with a gun, but still the money
got away—
the sale of the Stradivarius
dwarfed by the true price

        of Warley Place
        or rather, your love of it.
        Your white blood cells
        clustered and decayed.
        The head gardener did his duty
        and blew his brains. Your vision
        was reclaimed.

Molehills

Earth crumbles
out of itself, soft
as rumour, building

                      into a friable
                      breathing blot
                      on the lawnscape

        as a helpless
        vagrant, fumbling
        at unreachable air, leaves

                            a trail
                            of poor
                            punctuation

            blind
            to the spoiled
            vista of manicured grass.

      Insert
      batteries and tap
      home these tapered sonic poles—

warning: moles
may at first be attracted
through perverse curiosity.

            Scrape away
            soil to find the hole
            then pour in gulps of sump oil

and diesel
until the ground
seals with a repulsive glug;

      try gas—
      the sibilant echo
      of a hushed-up purge

         or light
         a stubby fuse and
         smoke the little fuckers.

  A neighbour
  stands poised
  with an iron spike;

        another
        digs at the speed
        of churning light—reaches

    into the dark
    for one trespasser
    and shuttles to the bottom

of the field,
offering a cruel,
temporary reprieve.

Ladybirds

Wobbling at the top of an aluminium ladder, he sliced through the laurel with his father's shears. Evergreen clippings took off around his face, and from the thick of it, a pigeon, with scissoring wings. Bright drops of blood on the pale green undersides of the leaves he saw were ladybirds, at which he breathed again, but set about his task with greater care, though he was up against time. The sky was darkening. Fat pearls of water gathered on the shrinking hedge like a swarm of little ghosts.

English Pastoral

The memory is a silent film—
driving south on a cloistered road
through rich wet Gloucestershire farmland.

At first I hardly noticed them—
each milestone a straw-flecked
                                              clod
fallen from the blade
                  of a plough.

Then I saw they were badgers—too many dead
for a coincidence, the cause instead
some savage new cowardice
more self-important than the law, run amok.

I hadn't the stomach
                          to stop and inspect
the gathering flies' sickly critique
of what was rotten, time
                          though to form
my own prejudice.

                This was England.

                            Now.

Christmas Diptych

I lug my chosen chopped spruce pine
into the barn and melted snow
forms dark puddles on polished stone.
Baubles are unwrapped, hung. I know
how tinsel must follow
                        the trail
of candles that thread a soft light
through feathered green
                             but the whole chain
of bulbs begins to flicker, fail,
and something
                falls—a gilded bird.
I try to relocate its perch
but every attempt is just plain
wrong, and the final effect—search
as I may for another word—
drab. I'm wishing it would come right

when I hear a distant voice draw
my gaze to the grevillea
in her front yard. I shield my eyes
from the December sun, and try
to make out the source of her joy:
something half-hidden and so still
I see it merely as a toy
until it flaps its green surprise
of leaf-like wings.
A dozen more
little lorikeets light the bush
with flashes of red—such a thrill
that I reach for my camera
and miss the whole carolling rush
into inimitable sky.

PART 2

In their entwined sleep they exchanged arms and legs
In their dreams their brains took each other hostage

In the morning they wore each other's face
                              —Ted Hughes, 'Lovesong'

La Tempesta
Giorgione, Gallerie dell'Accademia di Venezia

A lightning flash over the lagoon
displaces me—we're running again
headlong down
the flight of blinding stone
steps, towards noon,
grabbing a cup of iced red melon
before we adjourn

> to the cool interior
> of the Scuola della Carità,
> straight to the one picture
> you insist that I see: *La Tempesta*.
> All I can do is mumble, stutter,
> struck first by water
> the same thick blue-green texture

of the canal,
and imagine the same smell
drifting from a stagnant pool
five centuries old. Only then do I feel
the centrifugal pull
of the strange, anonymous couple
seemingly in exile

or on the run
—from what?—war-torn
European ruin?—
or Renaissance Eden?
They have no option
but to indulge their own
residual swagger or quotidian

demands—she to pause,
remove her dress
and lay it on the grass
as if this questionable bliss
were still Paradise.
She sits and outstares
whoever so much as dares

to raise an eyebrow at her wild
demeanour, her excuse the need
to suckle her child
but she's *nude*—
her legs lazily spread—
with only her shoulders shawled
as if against the cold

or a guard's approbation,
while her man, urbane,
but with gypsy skin,
cocky in his two-tone
stockings, seems almost to grin
as the storm crackles on,
knowing they must remain

        exactly as the artist painted the scene,
        their passion
        at once revealed and forbidden;
        both public domain
        and private garden
        lit like Golgotha, but serene;
        an omen.

        *

        You came here before, one bone-
        chilling winter, with reason
        to be alone;
        fell for the out-of-season
        muted strain
        of rich desolation;
        fell, like a noble Venetian,

for this painting, its blend
of sky, water and land
in colours illumined
by the storm. Now you stand
in your own footsteps and find,
perhaps, reaching for my hand,
how we might spend

> a life of love and subterfuge,
> making a silent pledge
> to hold our own selves hostage,
> venturing to the very edge
> of who we are. We enter the image
> and wait for the deluge...
> The deserted bridge

takes no-one anywhere.
The lightning is little more
than a chalky tear
in the cloud, a razored blur—
but it dragged us here
to witness how the viewer
has most to fear

       and we wait, stoic
       as that enigmatic stork
       on the roof, for the storm to break—
       electric baroque
       still decades away—stark
       staring mad for thinking the crack
       in the foreground is a snake,

or giddy still from the vaporetto,
thinking there's a shadow...
a faint, human glow
that lives within the *pentimento,*
managing to show
how even depicted happenings can flow...
And so

       it is that I learn
       of the other woman,
       the one the artist chose to drown
       beneath new layers of green
       and brown—
       never to explain
       why, or elucidate her pain.

We re-emerge from the small room,
stumbling from studied gloom
into day. The storm
has passed but lingers as a dream
        in spacetime
sharpening our sun-blazed form
to a bold continuum.

        *

        Our planes
leave in different directions
        but hit the same turbulence
and we plummet—sense
        a simultaneous
veering terror and stolid confidence
        as we glance

from separate cabin windows
        at the cloud, a canvas
stretched beneath us
        into the future, the noise
of the engine relentless
        as a rumbling loss
while we advance.

Venetian Lullaby
(for MZ)

You gaze from your cot at the belltower
of St Mark's. It seems only yesterday
that your mother was as small,
                                 but tonight
she holds the wooden lagoon in her palm—
twists the lumpen metal key, winds it tight
until the miniature gondolier
is released in an operatic mime,
gliding under the Rialto bridge. Our
frail memories are in his custody,
like a circling dream,
                           and in the minute
it takes for him to falter, stall,
                              you fall
for his solid, inscrutable charm,
                                steer
your own course through our commotions and let
your heavy eyelids close like a secret.

Transpositions

#1

You find your grandfather listed
as *colonial engineer*—a second life

shaping the future of an island town
towards the end of the earth,

a wind-scoured outpost of sheep,
brightened by its red tin roofs

and edible berries of diddle dee.
You wonder what possessed him—

taking his daughters, leaving his son
to years of lonely boarding school,

and when war came, marshalling
a home guard so far from home.

#2

Step from the car into the snow
and feel the chill through your boots.

You were heading for Yosemite
but you're miles adrift on a pass

they should have shut,
and what you thought was dusk

is nearer night, the blank ground
sparkling, showing you the way

to where a mountain lion lopes
into the dark, deep woods

and you don't yet understand
that you're a changeling, following.

#3

Months at sea become hours
in flight. Your morning cakewalk

through pinewoods to the beach
shifts at the stroke of a key

to an evening trek in the bush,
blackbirds turned currawongs

yodelling among the scribbly gums,
heading to where the ocean

smashes its unfamiliar blue
not against Old Harry and his wife

but rocks more treacherous, voiced
with mantic love; claiming you.

And when—

after your lifelong draw
to the north—
you veered so far
and wildly south
that your night
became day (and vice

versa),
it seemed a betrayal, but
the molten core—
the magnetic field
beneath your feet—
was revealed
as the traitor.
You had followed the law.

Here and There
(for KG)

That first year I travelled like a tourist,
agog at the Opera House, the giant fruit bats
in the botanical gardens, and the calm
of mile after slowly changing mile as I drove

under the singing skies, skies that redefined
my sense of space, redefined the colour blue
and what it could do for the human spirit.
Blue fairy wrens and blue satin bowerbirds

were my new companions. Stars
were doubly bright, and when two of them
formed eyes above the smile of the moon,
what could I do but smile in return?

It was three weeks in when the simple road
through the goldfields became a muddle
and I stopped, lost. Above me, a cockatoo
perched on a bare branch, mocking my search

for a sign. *Maldon* was all I asked, but map
and plan were no longer in accord. The run
of perfect, adventurous days had given way
to the tiresome quotidian: reason for turning

back, accepting that travel is rarely more
than a provisional life; but reason, too,
for believing that a new world could be home,
much like the troublesome, intractable old.

Carnarvon Gorge

Even in kilometres I had it
all worked out: the mileage of adventure
and the necessary weight of water
that would metamorphose from pure burden
into relief. Turquoise dragonflies looped
through the scintillating heat, their carefree
gossamer calculations beyond me
as I watched my step, following each stone
laid down, but still tempted by every
sidetrack, every glimpse of the unknown.

Was I half-way there?
                        Half way home?
                                          Either
way, I was exhausted,
                panicked.

                                      I scooped
a hatful of water from the river

over my head.

            Was this it?

                              My limit?

Four Seasons in One Day

The roof tiles of the Opera House glint
like late frost against a midsummer sky.
When a sudden wind startles the water
we duck inside. Two Bellinis later
the air is electric, the sky like flint.
The Spring brides, posing on the harbour front,
hold back their veils and pretend not to cry.
When you ask me if I can run, I smile

then kiss you—out of the blue—and leg it
around the famous horseshoe quarter mile
of slippery flagstones in the minute
before the theatre doors close. The curtain
rises on an Autumn sunset, serene.
You're still standing there, breathless, in the rain.

One midsummer night

she was finally nagged
into the yard to find him
the common possum
he had not seen—
caught in the lamplight

like Bathsheba Everdene,
her dress snagged
by the spurred boot
on Sergeant Troy's foot.

Sightings

Crimson Rosella

Blue winged angel, you tilt
into the drag and uplift of air,
feathering your feathers
into a tattered cross
gilded in afternoon sun

angled through the forest,
and settle on a eucalypt bough—
the curling capital letter
of an illuminated manuscript.

(Bruce, May 2016)

Superb Fairy-wren

There you go again—half-
seen miniature spectacular
inhabiting the scrub
above the river,
a twitching hallucination

whose flitterings
of superlative, hi-vis blue
are twitched by themselves—
can't do it, can't stay still!

(Kanimbla, December 2014)

Wedge-tailed Eagle

You draw invisible, slow
circles, drifting in the sky,
bafflingly high above
suburban rooftops—
so high that your focus

is elsewhere, wired
to a few scrabbling pixels
at large in a patch
of neighbouring bush.

(Bruce, March 2016)

Short-tailed Shearwater

Mutton bird—the indignity
of being named after your taste!
You plummet and glide
through water like silk—
but landing? Landing

is an embarrassing crash
in the deliberate dark,
desperate to burrow
your velvet into the night.

(Heron Island, December 2008)

Australian Magpie

Singly, in pairs, or like today,
out in force, policing
the grassy precinct
in case of a flashmob riot
of your own making,

you walk the walk, talk
the talk and corroborate
in secret cahoots
your black and white point.

(Bruce, May 2016)

Red-rumped Parrot

What a conjuring trick!—
your bright greens rummaging
on drab green verges
somehow camouflaged,
yellow belly mottling the ground

like a turning leaf, all thrown
to the wind as you open
your wings and show
your blooming show-off rump.

(Bruce, May 2016)

Superb Lyrebird

You shy away, trek deeper
into the forest, scratching
for scratchings in the mulch
of twigs, echoing
your own progress—

rustling up a dusty music
from every scuff of dirt
and giving voice
to the skiffle of your feet.

(Barrington Tops, December 2013)

Blue-winged Kookaburra

From across the still water
of Black Rock Falls,
where the merest glint
of pale-blue silver is perched
on a hairline fault

in the glistening, vertical
black rock, comes
the ancient silver cackling
of your long-distance laugh.

(Kununurra, December 2011)

Rainbow Pitta

You gleam in the shadow
of the lightning man,
with turquoise epaulettes
luminous against the ochres
of Kakadu's late afternoon

and the gathering thick
black Kakadu clouds,
an electric premonition
of life after the storm.

(Nourlangie, December 2011)

Turtles

Watching you head out
of the Portrait Gallery,
cello strapped to your back
in its foam-lined polymer shell,
I see how—the time I took

a fiddle on my Harley
to a gig in the cathedral—
I was an Eastern Long Neck
blinking at all that peopled light.

The Shallows

You break from the company
of sharks and swim leisurely
to shore; such a simple task—
stepping from one paradise
to another—but you falter,

faced with picking your way
through the shovelnose
and cowtail rays that bask
in the next-to-nothing water.

Heron Island

2011–2008

Half-awake, stumb-
        ling onto the beach, we almost trip over them:
                        shadows taking form

as each exhausted loggerheaded limb
                hauls its loggerheaded bulk through the gloom

and follows the strange magnetism
        of birth; turtles spurred on by the multi-male jism
                in their hold—irrepressible, blundering sperm—

channelling the momentum
            of that easy pull through the sea into this tortuous climb

to higher ground, this lumb-
        ering pantomime, all in the name of the slim
                slim chance of their cargo also laying claim

to it as home. I was here once before. There was a storm

that arrived with an all-night dawn
   chorus I couldn't get out of my head, an amplified, twittering drone

—the whole island a boombox of birds—gone
                      by the first premonition
                                  of pale, ineffectual sun,

heavy in the sky like a stone.
               I took a snap of a lone
                          turtle twisting towards the receding shoreline

before I saw how one
          flipper was missing in action.
                                  By the jetty, a single white heron

kept watch as I waited for the catamaran.
                          Already I felt the urge to return
                                        with offspring of my own

and as I stepped once more from deck
                        to shore, it all came back—
                                                the squawk

of nesting black
            noddies clustered close as thoughts, the air thick
                                                with the reek

of guano. Now there's a squeak
                    of white sand as I walk
                                        the blinding perimeter track

in thirty minutes. I watch you float with a shark
    mere inches from your nose. Later, you keep vanishing for a smoke,

burdened with a knowledge that will have to take
                        its chances with the rest. I pick
                                a silver turtle to hang around your neck

like a charm, and recall how the flippers scooped
                              a sandy pit
                                       and formed a chute

from which to divulge a flow of eggs like a secret,
                    shells flexing against the fall in a single wet

clutch. I wonder if I could bear it—
                    after an eighty-day wait—
              to watch even one scampering hatchling run the gauntlet

like a D-Day recruit.
          Meanwhile heron and turtle face off on the waterfront.
                                                  I take the brunt

of your accusations, fail to acquit,
          and in the struggle to say something careful, *just right*,
                                                  blurt it all out.

Twice now the outward adventure

so much safer than the return.
I watch the sky blacken
with oily fumes from the struggling engine.
A barefooted girl—close enough to stern
for me to imagine her blown
overboard—stretches her arms to align
with the shocking tilt of the horizon,
fixing her gaze while everyone

else huddles inside to endure
the grim interminable hour before
we reach shore.
                      She tells me it's the sure-fire
way to cope. I try to copy, fail, hold instead to *her*—
this girl, whose youthful wisdom I admire
so much that I still conjure
                                  her levelling allure.

How could he have known—

watching the English surf pool
around his toes, safe in the lee
of the bolted timber groyne
and his mother within sight,
chatting to a friend—

how a different, wild white sea
would throw him, more frail
for thinking he could stand
on his own two grown-up feet?

An act of love

was how he thought of it—leaving his arm
wrapped under her, the clamminess
of cooling sweat welding them
like a dream,
               the slight numbness
in his fingers a pleasure, deepening
into tolerable pain,
                    then gone.
He couldn't bear to wake her—had pledged
himself to hold her through the night—
but enough became enough, and when
he finally eased himself loose
                           he found
all feeling lost, saw—in the opening
space between them—his own lifeless
flesh,
    a cold white bodypart dredged
from the sea. He lifted its alien

density with his operable hand
and it seemed like minutes before he sensed
the arm begin to quibble with itself,
pins versus needles, his reviving nerves
like a nest of cheerful, squabbling chicks
not knowing what to do with their new lives
except jostle and squeal for attention.
And as she turned, startled, he tensed:

what option but to share this gibberish
with her slowly dawning disbelief—
watching his fingers once again flex—
that instead of hungering for more sleep or sex
he was even bothering to explain
something hardly worth the mention.

Touch

Afterwards, on a quiet, midday stroll
through a wood, he was startled as a bird—
so close it almost brushed against his face—
burst from the dry eucalypt foliage,
tail feathers shaped to a perfect fan
with white tips backlit by silvering sun,
and as it disappeared into the sky
his hand stretched out, helpless, as if to reach
once again
            for the delicate white lace
of a blue nightdress, lifting from her thigh,
thinking he might yet bring that privilege
back into his own domain,
                          but he heard—
like a terror, rasp
            -ing his very soul—
her gasp
      of pleasure at another's touch.

His deceptive memory

has it as Good Friday
when he pulled up outside
the reserve and saw
how a kangaroo
had jumped the wire but

somehow caught its foot
and hung there like a hide.
The vision is still raw.
That much at least is true.

Ply

She takes a plain circular board, primes it, sands it,
primes again, re-sands, wanting it so white—
so smooth—that its pure blank hungers
for her painterly thoughts.

She clamps it on her easel, mixes a favourite
deep turquoise wash on her palette,
but her loaded brush then lingers
in the air—a quiet small boy in yellow shorts

distracting her, like a long-forgotten photograph
suddenly recalled; as if she's known him all her life,
this boy—solitary on a distant shore
she has yet to mark out

on her immaculate void—staring across half
a century, into her eyes. With her knife,
she presses new colours to her task: more
paint; more urgency; more doubt.

*

    It was nothing
more than plywood,
     a thin but firm piece
of wood that wasn't wood at all
     but glued layers of veneer
rotated when stacked
     so that the wafered grain
was coloured like a biscuit
     his father sawed by hand
into a yard-wide perfect circle
     sanded until its surface
was like glass, varnished
     in layers of toughening shine,
so that when it was cast
     onto the remnant of the tide
it skimmed along the beach
     on a film of sandy water
and as he ran and planted
     his two bare feet
and next-to-nothing weight
     on the board just right
it gained the brief momentum
     of unsimulated joy

       *

A pale, full moon darkens under cloud.
Soft clogged bristles drag like the tide—
like gentle stubble across skin; sandpapery
drifts that lay down a glistening sediment,

each brushstroke a visionary act, pigment
as faith, and somewhere—at the periphery
of her circling gaze—that silent figure in a slide
toward the centre, but his presence is too loud,

too troubled. She wraps him in the colours
and movements of the sea, blurs
his diminutive form until only a faint patch
of yellow remains, like sunlight on sand.

And now what—all too little? too bland?
She puts it aside for a time when her touch
will blend him back in such a way that stirs
her own imaginings: steadfast; tremulous.

To think—

how you loved
her dreamy imperfection,
her lazy eye, her subtle lisp
that rendered every word
a seduction,
good
as a kiss
or the precise caress

that never reached you,
even though your skin
would yearn
for it, through
every waking hour
of every sleepwalking year.

Page 147[*]

Paint her to your own mind—
a simultaneous demand
for secrecy and the broad,
daylight gestures of rejoice,

a love letter in invisible ink,
not knowing who will look
through ultraviolet eyes
and understand

or shrug their shoulders
and choose instead
to rub a coloured
crayon over the indented

contours of the page to crack
this childlike code.

---

[*] 'To conceive this right, —call for pen and ink—here's paper ready to your hand, —Sit down, Sir, paint her to your own mind—as like your mistress as you can—as unlike your wife as your conscience will let you—'tis all one to me—please but your own fancy in it.'
    —Laurence Sterne, *Tristram Shandy, Vol VI*

The King Lear Catalogue, 1976–2015

You scrunch your blond hair clear
of your face as we enter the theatre.
I think of Caravaggio's David
doing something similar with Goliath's head
that day in the Prado gallery, Madrid,

Cap'n Barbosa winking at me eight years
before I'd see him here, as one of many Lears,
almost passing out in the upper balcony
as eyes turn to jelly; in Stratford

John Nettles was the Duke of Albany
before a life of *Midsomer Murders*,
Bob Peck as Kent, pre-Jurassic Park;

and that pretender to the throne, in York,
pre-echoing Timothy West's every word.

Muldoonery

Seven plus years from finding myself lost
on the outskirts of Maldon,
I've come to a quayside room
in Sydney

witnessing Muldoon
contend with a raucous espresso machine.
'Keeping Going' is his best
tribute to Heaney

as a helicopter's wallop
overhead enables him to weave,
like a magician,

each chop
of air into that heavy duty poem
about the troubles. I leave,

remembering how, in Chicago,
he became transfixed
by his left-of-stage accomplice,
who like a sword-swallower

took those quicksilver
turns of phrase
and re-delivered them with death-defying physics
to an audience that began to gasp

at this curious sideshow:
the slightly nervous, mid-delivery glance
from the maestro

and the virtuoso
dextrous response
that even non-deaf listeners could grasp.

PART 3

The blood jet is poetry,
There is no stopping it.
—Sylvia Plath, 'Kindness'

Tethered

Beneath the pantiled roof, joists, rafters,
    insulating foam...

Beneath the humdrum conversation...

Beneath the soft wool pile of the rug...

Beneath the woven seagrass
    bonded to its rubber underlay...

Beneath the concrete screed...

Beneath the visqueen membrane
    keeping down the damp...

Beneath the hardcore, the rubbled brick,
    blinded with sand...

And tethered to a tethering ring of iron
    bolted into bedrock...

A shred of rotting, tethering rope
    grimed with blood

And the muffled squeal that won't let go.

Fire

Fuse

a strike... a spark... a sputtering wish... a procrastination... a shiver of sunlit wind through leaves... a chalked line drawn across the board, towards whiskey's lingering scorch... a scorpion on an anthill... a whispered intimation of calamity or hurrah... the colossal bridge splintering to matchsticks... horses falling in slow motion into the river... ribbons of blood... the long, long haul to retribution and beyond...

On Egdon Heath

He lies in a bed of crisping bracken—bracken straight out of the book he's discarded in the sun. He takes a magnifying glass from his pocket, focuses on the crinkled fronds. A half-hidden lizard squirms at the intrusion that grows to a torrid inquisition. He senses the power he has to ratchet up the heat into a crime. His own skin is darkening. Unread pages of the novel begin their incendiary curl.

Fahrenheit 451

One toy in particular he remembers, motoring over the carpet, with a yellow ladder you could wind as high as... as high as the TV... its astonishing feat to reverse from every collision—with chair leg, skirting board, coal scuttle, cat—and set off on a new mission... in the age when everyone—much as they needed rescuing—seemed safe. There it is, still wound up, or batteried, he can't remember which, nosing into trouble and saving the day. Bright red, like in a film...

1 February 1829

His brother might have painted it, a scene of damnation, but he—he wanted his hellfire more real. He sat through evensong, fingering the razor in his pocket, sick of the priests' buzzing nonsense in his ear, then hid in the belltower until dark: shredded the velvet in the Bishop's pew; piled it high with cushions and hymn books and set it alight. Grabbing a bellrope, he swung through the minster window like a cartoon. And yes, they found him, tramping to the pub, fragments of flint and stained glass in his pockets—but he was adamant: *Not me, my lord, but my God is guilty.*

Visionary

Some nights, by the hearth, he thought he saw blue-green phantoms within the flames. And one morning, sitting in the big bay window of his parents' room, when they were elsewhere (where?), he watched a hummingbird come to the glass, its frantic wings—like blurred rainbows—enabling it to hang, poised in the air... but he lived on the wrong continent, no-one believed him, and later, when his mind wasn't right, he wondered if that had been the case all along, that he'd been seeing things. The thought torched his world like a burning bush.

Alphabet Jigsaw

I spread the cut-out shapes
on your bedroom floor
and do my best
to help with the simplest:
a for apple, g for grapes...

but you keep homing in
on r for rainbow
and x—'a sort of photo'
you call *the man with no skin*.

Bring Me the Head

The siege at Trencher's Farm
plays out: the man-trap
hanging above the fire;
Sam with pneumonia
brought on by a month
of Cornish damp,
mixed with a chronic

        consumption of scotch.
        His mind is on *Garcia*,
        four films down the line,
        though he'll never see it
        for the self-portrait
        it will be. He beckons,
        and everyone leans

in for his tedious brief,
their verdict like yesterday:
Complete Waste of Time.
Fugue, he mumbles
when he latches on,
but hasn't the strength
to hurl more abuse,

        let alone the knife
        that's already splintered
        the cupboards. Some poor fool
        has to score this shambles
        with 'something ironic'
        and when the sketched-in
        Stravinsky fits the bill

it's simply left there
with the ratcatcher's giggles.
Sam's new Girl Friday
is the one who smuggles
him more booze
but nobody will own up
to knowing anything at all

        about the misshapen lump
        from which a dark blotch
        is seeping through the canvas
        bag by his sick-bed,
        beginning to attract flies:
        possibly a rotting beetroot;
        possibly not.

Camille
(for PH)

Six months of absence blurred into seven, accompanied by relentless rain. Mud took control. The house was in danger of sliding down the mountain into Grauman's Chinese, and still her husband stayed away. Her mind filled with the grotesque, seeing him let rip into Mexican whores in tandem with Sam, all their wild cronies roaring them on. She saw her marriage in the racing sludge, every slug of tequila. Her sanity began to slip. She sat in the dark, looking out over the city, preparing her tirade, laughing at her own innocence, laughing at the charade of writing music in the desert—for *seven fucking months*. She began to compose a soundtrack of her own: carefully orchestrated shrieks and sobs to welcome him home.

Meringue

Years later, when her spoon touched his, dipping into the creamed meringue, she thought how it might have been so good. Perhaps it had been, and this civility was the charade. The bottle empty, they sat in silence, wondering how long the waiter might take to bring them the bill, if they should split it, or if some initiative beyond their known competence might be required.

Country House Visitor, Yorkshire, c. 1996

He woke to a morning perfectly still:
a lazy mist rising in the garden;
a grey heron poised at the water's edge,
intent. He slipped quietly downstairs to plunge,
naked, into the over-heated pool.

Over time, he would return to the scene:
how she blundered in, armed with a towel
not wanting though to linger but to urge
him on his way; how he felt such a fool
as he threw his bag into the car, turned

on the gravel drive and saw the heron
lift, stall and sprawl—just as he heard the gun—
legs hanging slack like electric cable,
sparks of bright blood flumping into the pond.

Macbeth

(for KM) Bubwith, Yorkshire, June 2016

Lady Macduff, so beautiful, so young, is delaying proceedings; it's her first day, she's worried about her hair. There are whispers... Another ten minutes. Someone puts a red cross on the far, green wall. Thick wires spill from the camera. Finally, she reappears, her hair the same perfection it was before. I want to tell her how little it matters, but my presence means nothing. It's as if I'm not there.

*

We adjourn for lunch in a grassy courtyard. There's a net, strung between the two barns where everyone sleeps. Fleance has found a playmate, and flicks the shuttlecock up towards the sun. It speeds from his racquet, then stalls. The breeze is against him, and as the shuttlecock falls into the net, then falls again, his friend losing patience, I have to keep telling myself that it's just a game.

*

As I drive away, I catch a glimpse of Macbeth in his leather skirts, standing in the middle of the country lane to catch a signal. He waves one hand in the air as he talks—perhaps to his wife; the other is clutched to the side of his head, and I imagine the blood from his ear now smeared on his mobile. The sun is out. The roof is back and I hear clear birdsong above the engine's hum and the rubbery grind of tyres through the dust. Trees in full leaf rush towards me on both sides.

*

The pall bearers heave the draped corpse to their shoulders, then wait, while people stare at the geometry on screen, pointing fingers. Faces, now familiar, form a corridor through which the body must pass. The Macbeths, at the head of the lines, lean in to share a secret joke. The children look nervous. Someone adjusts the fall of the cloth, asks one line of mourners to move in: six inches. More. Stop. Now there's a perfect vanishing point. A bell rings. The cortège begins its slow, slow shuffle. The screen is toggled from green to black.

*

There are some with very little to do. Really very little. The First Murderer, for instance: next to nothing. Four weeks in and his whiskied nights have grown into whiskied days. He's no longer good company. And his face—his face now looks bruised from within, and the ever-blackening bags under his eyes are carrying a sickness. But this morning, as he hauls his self-brutalised body from his bed, he's finally summoned, and the method in his madness uncoils like a snake. He's sharp, word-perfect, dressed to kill.

*

Life intervenes; death, rather. We wait in the boxed pews, with organ music faintly out of tune. In the front row, grandchildren, generations adrift from the white-haired assembly behind them. As the tributes begin, I think of the absent body, burnt or buried months ago. I think of the dummy carried from Dunsinane under a grey cloth. I hear a sound that could be the soft popping of a microphone, that is actually raindrops falling through the defective lead of the church roof. I think of tomorrow: Banquo's ghost. We adjourn to the inevitable feast.

Fair Bianca
(for JH)

Forty years after he last saw her, she died. It was the first thing he read, on waking, alone, on the other side of the world. A chain of emails, all with 'no words'. And so he offered none in return. But the silence rankled: he thought how disease could be written through the body like a stick of rock, and nobody know; how a youthful infatuation could be the same. He thought of forty years with nothing said; the accrual of silence like rust in a lock. And when words finally came to him, they weren't his own, but those remembered, rehearsed: *I saw her coral lips to move, And with her breath she did perfume the air; Sacred and sweet was all I saw in her.*

Midsummer, Brownsea, 1965

The island picnic morphs
into a play, peacocks strolling
across the woodland stage, alive
to their new-found, haunting fame.
The moonlit ferry home

is a lingering dream,
flowerdrops on our eyelids a balm
against the terrifying
counter-narratives; the rebuffs.

Freckle
(for CM)

No-one could explain away
the growing freckle in your eye.

You had to offer it up
for closer scrutiny in the lab,

lose a precious five-minute slice
of your blue-grey iris—

the same captivating muscle
that sought my approval

as I sat opposite you, stunned.
All I could do was nod

and come the hour, cradle a glass
of single malt, Joplin's *Solace*

playing in my head as if my jitter
was part of a romantic caper

to get back at the world.
I saw my shaky hands—gnarled,

scrubbed of their workaday dirt
by an amateur; thought

how tomorrow the surgeon
would want you to sign

the intimidating form of consent
to procedures different

to the plan, should anything
go wrong...

which doesn't happen. Instead,
when you wake—the cotton pad

removed from your face—
he finds some further trace

of imperfection, a flaw
in his own craft. You outstare

the glint of the blade as it
dips into the white

of your eye like an egg
and I watch, helpless, ache

with feeble, visceral fear
of what is now no more

than a pitiful irrelevance,
the need for reassurance

that there is nothing, my love,
nothing to be afraid of.

The Weathercock

The iron weathervane needed new paint. Someone brought it down from the coach house roof—my father? Braving that height, before he fell ill? (For me, the rooftop was the sky.) The cockerel perched on the lawn, and I scraped the flaking black from its north, south, east and west with a stiff wire brush, then daubed it with glistening enamel: scarlet beak and comb, gold feathers. I liked it there, left within reach, though it did no more than creak this way and that, bereft of the high winds that gave it true direction. Suddenly I see it's me, stuck there, gormless, aloof, waiting for my father to haul things back.

The Larder

Sometimes I still wander in
as if foraging for breakfast,
finding cereals labelled
in shillings and pence,
their flat-pack
African animal heads
like grotesque butterflies

      waiting to metamorphose.
      The instructions are simple—
      fold tab A over tab B
      and pass X through the slots
      as shown in figure 1—
      but I no longer want
      their boxy 3D trophy stares.

I shake a different packet
and a miniature diver
falls with the edible dust
into my bowl. He only needs
a pinch of baking powder
in the tank on his back
to initiate the miracle—

        the slow drift down
        through a glass of water
        where reactionary bubbles
        haul him to the surface
        before he tilts and repeats
        the whole mysterious
        cycle of recall—

but the tub is empty.
I search the higher shelves,
aimlessly now, feeling
along the slightly rusty top
of the green metal meat safe
where there's no reason
to put anything, but that

        is where I find it, an old tin
        of pastilles, which rattles
        as I prise open the lid
        and swallow hard,
        looking at a dozen or so
        immaculate specimens:
        my once milky white teeth.

See—

how quotidian
tiredness
leads to calamitous fatigue,
wears the body down
like a rumour
entering a league
of its own
(your skin as witness)—

how the hidden
tumour
takes its cue
from such success
and all you can do
is embody the duress.

In the Capuchin catacomb

clothed bodies are pegged
to the wall, mouths clogged
with the dust of their own skin
but within a whisker of some-
how letting us tune in

to their patient utterance
or casting a sidelong glance
at our shuffling, grey-shawled
capitulations, appalled.

Chromatic

A frisson—discovering the composer
was a murderer: Gesualdo, Prince of Venosa.

It was thrilling as pornography:
imagine—finding your wife *in flagrante*

delicto and doing the butchery
yourself—a baby

into the bargain, possibly your own.
I was just twelve, curious to learn

how the wife (and cousin), Maria d'Avalos,
had lost two previous husbands from *excess*

of connubial bliss.
I could feel the dark harmonies

taking my body to a new, strange place,
each exotic chord change a pass

through the arras... 'How now! a rat?'
The smell of rotting meat

guides a shark to the scene
through currents of formaldehyde green

into which, as the protein
in its eye will eventually tell, it was born

four centuries ago,
around the time Caravaggio

was on the run for murder and *Macbeth*
in rehearsal. *The physical impossibility of death*

is its secret for as long as another polar bear
falls through the ice, although a fire

in the Galapagos
saw a near immortal giant tortoise

swing through the air
like Dick Fosbury clearing the bar

with his why-not technique
that would give everyone the knack:

Lucy in Syracuse, with diamonds in her skull,
singing a modern madrigal

even as a painting lowers her remains
into a subterranean vault—bones

that will bide their time until
her saint/celebrity DNA merits a revival.

I copy the score in my shaky hand
and begin to understand

why an artist signs his name in the blood
pooling from a prophet's head.

A Footnote

And when her menstrual blood
kicked in, and they had fucked,
he would push a piece of bread
into her cunt to be soaked
in both of their seed

and he would eat it.
It was what he asked—
along with the occasional request
to be kissed, or to be held.

Four Poster

The frame was hung with tapestries. If he lay
on the bed and stretched his arms and legs
towards the corners he could almost imagine
a quartering of himself, a bloody severance

*

and what possessed her ? the time she scattered
rose petals in between the sheets, so that when
they regained their senses they also reeled
from the crimson stains that suggested a gross

*

bereavement, and since none of the four
children could house the legacy whole, the bed
was dismembered, the individual, equal limbs
allotted to separate homes, like orphans

*

this one drilled for a red and black flex to run
through its hollowed mahogany core
like an artery, powering the electric light
where I sit at night and witness its first flickers.

Fractures

The pub shut down; neighbourly disagreements
went to ground. Now, at harvest, rifts
rehearse their muscular subterranean flux
with ice-cold wine in the old schoolhouse, farmers

*

who needs them—and that soft-spoken gardener
is the one who stole the ten-year woodpile
from your field. You seriously consider
setting fire to his house as a form of poetic

*

impotence was what the solicitor called it
when news of his wife's affair was forcibly planted
in his brain. He calmly took his gun and shot her
dog, which was the final straw, the whole village

*

divided in its outrage, mouthing off words
that were all too connived, debased, toxic; a body
politic reeling from some seismic blow job,
its blind eye not knowing which way to turn.

redruM

Their naked bodies, kneeling
in secular prayer, were shadows
playing on the wall,
but turning
his head he saw the full

technicolour act for what it was,
crudely overwritten in thick
strokes of scarlet lipstick
on the sliding mirror doors.

Steadicam

TRACKING SHOT. INTERIOR.
Danny, pedalling in the corridor
of the Overlook Hotel, the only sound
the rumble of wheels, muffled
by carpet. CUT TO: EXTERIOR:

Danny, placing one foot after another
into his own snow-hollow prints...
backwards... no room for error...
his life in the balance.

All Work and No Play

Clattering through the lobby—
the quick-action strikes
of a repetitive axe
whittling your self to a stack
of fractional mistakes: Jakc

a... dlllboy... this your hobby—
battering out these indented
letters on the page, demented
as any splintering affray.

The Bulmer Murder

The story of Captain John Bolton of Bulmer, near Castle Howard, accused of murdering Elizabeth Rainbow, his apprentice girl, a single woman, at the parish of Bulmer in the county of York on the 21st day of August, 1774.

Sunday, 21st of March, 2008

I was shifting a barrow
of earth across the garden
to relieve one clog of land
and replenish another.
The wind had got up,
and with it the strange
swift tilt of time:

> the familiar low sun
> of late afternoon; the sky
> thickening with layers
> of black, the backdrop
> for a bending spectrum
> of light—a double rainbow
> ghosting itself

into the garish orange
of pantiled roof
and the electric green
of wet, lit grass;
the whole village
coloured like the glass
windows of its church.

I had stumbled
on your story, the burden
of that barrow suddenly
forcing my hand.
A troubled sunset bled
its deepening red
into my eye.

A month later, 1774

   ELIZABETH SCAYLING. What age was Elizabeth Rainbow?—I cannot tell ; but ſhe has lived with him for ſix or ſeven years : When ſhe came to him ſhe was a little girl, about eight or ten years old.
   JANE TAYLOR (neighbour). I ſaid what did ſhe ail ; ſhe ſaid ſhe could not tell, but her legs ſwelled ; her miſtreſs was in the hall and heard us, and ſaid if ſhe was well to eat and work, there could be little the matter with her... She ſaid that when Mr Bolton or her went to York they muſt get ſomething for her, but ſhe was ſo ſtupid ſhe would not take it, though they got it. I thought it was the green-ſickneſs.
   THOMAS BUSFIELD (journeyman to Mr Garencler, apothecary, York): He [John Bolton] wanted an electuary making up, for which he had a preſcription... a preparation of ſteel... for removing obſtructions... dangerous to be given to a woman with child.

21st of August

Soon after three o'clock,
around the time that Cook
sails west of Pentecost
in the South Pacific,
Captain Bolton
sees his wife off to Foston
for tea with a friend.

>The Bowes boy
>is next, on an errand
>to Stittenham. It's a plan,
>surely, to have everyone
>out of the way,
>though perhaps for no more
>than the scheduled misdemeanour

of habitual adultery;
Betty his apprentice
in those breathless arts
of which nobody speaks.
What then happened
to press his hand
into something worse

than 'crime of passion'
could possibly suggest,
abominable, gross?
Even the speculation hurts.
What hours of cruelty
had turned into weeks?
What did she resist?

5 o'clock

EMANUEL BOWES. *When I got back... I turned the mare loofe in the yard, and went to the glafs door that opens into the orchard. I lift up the latch and found it faft... I went round to the ftreet door and knocked for near a quarter of an hour. William Mafterman, who lives oppofite, was fitting at his door with a child on his knee...*

WILLIAM MASTERMAN. *I laugh'd at him and faid, knock, 'Manuel, thy name's up (an old faying in our town). I then faw [Bolton] walking acrofs the yard, from the glafs-door towards the ftable.*

EMANUEL BOWES. *[My mafter] was very much in a flutter ; his hair stood upon end, and he had not his hat on... He bid me... go to Robert Boys about fome hay. When I came back... [my master] was fet by the fire in the parlour, drinking tea. He faid Emanuel, did you meet Betty on the road ; and I faid No, have you fent her an errand ; he faid fhe is run away... He faid while he came out at the glafs door to tell me to go to the Moor-houfes, fhe went out at the ftreet door, and he faw no more of her. I went into the kitchen. There was no Betty there.*

WILLIAM MASTERMAN. *[The ftreet door] never was opened all that time... nobody came out till fix o'clock when I went away.*

Earlier that day, 2014

I walk the two miles
to where you sent him, Bowes,
matching my every footstep
to the topography of the crime,
wondering where it was
that the cow doctor resided
as I struggle enough to find

        the two bed & breakfasts
        for our imminent guests.
        How was there time
        to dismantle a rainbow,
        consign the colours of a life
        into dirt? You can see
        directly from one hilltop

to the other—how a bonfire
might send its semaphore
of flame
across the valley,
its contours clouded
with an outback haze of flies
like documentary malingerers

wanting to know
how each passing year
and every underhand
second
becomes an accomplice
to the illusion of proof;
becomes proof.

Monday, 22nd of August, 1774

    EMANUEL BOWES. I got my breakfaſt about nine o'clock. My maſter came to me, and said, 'Manwell, you muſt get your ſpade, I have a job for you. I was to carry it into the orchard, and he would mark out the place where I was to take the earth. He ordered me to fill the wheel-barrow ; and I ſaw him lay the boards for the barrow to run through the hall to the cellar door ; I ſaw him throw the earth from the barrow into the cellar... he gave me the barrow to take back, and get ſome more ; he told me to throw it in at the cellar door and it fell down the ſteps ; when I had got about half a dozen barrow-fulls, I heard ſomebody in the cellar moving the dirt ; I kept wheeling on for about half a dozen more, about twelve in all. I wheeled every morning for a fortnight together...

Main Street, September, 1983

When I first set foot
through the front door
I found the kitchen sink
full of muddy water
as if someone had rinsed
the filth from their boots
and left the evidence

>as a dismal welcome.
>I couldn't but wonder
>at the nonchalance—
>like Bolton's, feet up
>by the fire after his labour,
>drinking his tea,
>then resting over a gate

three yards from his house,
calling to a neighbour
about some wood.
*How did he look?—as free
and hearty as ever I ſaw him
in my life.*
A few days later

he had the guts
to be back, the vendor,
thinking he could chop
more logs and set off
on a rant—kick up a stink
about townies convinced
they owned the damn place.

Prisoner's defence

JOHN BOLTON. *My reaſon for filling up the cellar was, that the water came in very faſt ever ſince it had been ſunk, which is near nine years ago : It came in ſo faſt that it hurt the foundation of the houſe, and part of it, at that end, fell in about two or three years ago. In the winter before laſt, my eldeſt son fell into it, when it was full of water, which made Mrs Bolton and myſelf ſo uneaſy, that I promiſed I would fill it up as ſoon as the cellar was dry. This declaration I made to several perſons ; and as ſoon as the cellar was dry, and hay-time over, I set about it, by giving directions to the lad, and telling him that he ſhould have the gardener to aſſiſt him...*

Now

When the water rises,
or I dig again, believing
there might come to light
some residual trace
of your act—a faint pigment
in the soil, a fragment
of bone or a microscopic hair

        of rope—I catch the echo
        of whatever melody
        once played on that fife
        before it was put
        to its gruesome last use.
        It's the same birdsong
        fills the evening air

as when you gathered
the lambs into your fold.
I listen and pick out
a tune on the piano
to redeem not your deed
but the tools of its trade:
the fife, the cord, the spade.

The tune is a *courante*:
she'd run away before;
you clung to the fantasy
that absolving your lies
she had done it once more;
all that grim stuff
of your hiding concealed.

5th of September, 1774

JOHN HALL. *When I went down the ſteps, they appeared like a ſlope bank with freſh earth... one corner [of the cellar] was filled with freſh earth within a little of the chamber joiſts...*

MARK RICHARDSON. *I took the ſhovel, and took a little of the earth, and found a ſtick. I gave it a pull, but found it faſt. I gave it a twiſt, and it broke. I ſaw ſome hair, and then I perceived her left arm, which ſeemed faſt. I then took my dig and pulled her up. Her arms were tied behind her back. There was a cord around her neck, and the other part of the fife was twiſted in the cord, and tied under her left arm. Was the body offenſive?—Very offenſive. I knew her before but ſhe was very much altered; her face was very much ſwollen, and of a blue colour.*

JOHN HALL. *We picked carefully about with his ſhovel and diſcovered her head.*

JOSEPH WEST (surgeon). *When I opened the body, I found a male foetus. About five months. I took off [the rope]. It was twice about, and twiſted with the fife. I examined the gullet with my finger, and found it twiſted in two.*

(undated)

Did you picture yourself
cohabiting with the dead?
You and your wife
with your child and lover
gagged forever
in the improvised graveyard
mere inches underfoot?

> Or did you know you would flee
> with a brace of pistols
> and the family silver
> bulging from your clothes,
> ready to buy your way
> to new trouble, new strife?
> I pretend it was me

with disintegrating victim,
sentenced for the term
of my natural life.
It's not hard to feel—
even from the other side
of the world—
the terrifying seal

of my lips as I doff my hat
to familiar strangers,
pass the time of day
with the comfort of untold
manageable dangers;
a dumb beast aware
at least of others in my care.

27th of March, 1775

THE HON. SIR HENRY GOULD, KNIGHT (His Majesty's Justice of the Court of Common Pleas). *The law has thought fit in great wiſdom to inflict a puniſhment upon perſons found guilty of a crime of this nature, which points out the heinouſneſs of the offence. This will happen when you are no more in this world. Conſider with yourſelf, and endeavour to find mercy, while there are any hopes of it. There is very little time for you to live in this world, but if you employ that time properly, you may find mercy from the Fountain of all mercies.*

The ſentence that the law obliges me to pronounce upon you is, That you, John Bolton, be led from this place from whence you came, and taken to the place of execution on Wedneſday morning, and hung by the neck till you are dead ; and after that your body to be diſſected and anatomized. God have mercy upon your ſoul!

Twilight, late millennium

What made me copy
this account of the trial
into my own dull-boy hand?
It became like a memory,
translating the poor facts
in all their muddied clarity
from sixpenny pamphlet

> into my new
> yellow notebook,
> every detail
> a fresh smudge
> verging on the bland;
> a discrepancy that distracts.
> And then?

What more to do
with the raw material
than idly retrace each
shape on the page,
allowing the *r*s to curl
over into *n*s and bear
witness to *Murder*

twisting into *Munden*,
feeling the whole gamut
of fear in my stomach;
the arrhythmic thump
of my drifting heart;
the concomitant lump
in my throat.

POSTSCRIPT. *During his trial, he behaved with a degree of boldneſs and unconcern, ſeldom to be diſcovered in perſons under ſuch circumſtances ; but when the cords and fife, with which the unfortunate girl was ſtrangled, were produced, his countenance fell, and he ſeemed greatly agitated. After the judge had ſolemly pronounced ſentence upon him he perſevered in his declaration, ſaying, in a manner that ſeemed to ſhock the whole court, by G-d, my lord, I am innocent.*

The next morning he was attended by two clergymen, and ſtill perſiſted in aſſerting that he was innocent ; they obſerved to him, that he had ſhocked the whole court, not only with the declaration of his innocence, but alſo with the manner in which he expreſſed it, which was foreign to the character he aſſumed: After having repeatedly conjured him to cloſe the ſcene with that behaviour becoming a ſincere penitent, they had the concern to leave him as they found him, obdurate.

Early on Wedneſday morning he found means to be his own executioner in the cell. He effected this, by tying a lift garter and a piece of cord that ſupported his irons to a handkerchief, the end of which he had fixed to a piece of wood, broke off from an old table in the cell, and put it through an air-hole : He was diſcovered between ſix and ſeven o'clock hanged, or rather ſtrangled, his feet being on the ground. The body was not cold. A ſurgeon was immediately ſent for, who open'd a vein, and he bled a little, but was too far gone to be recovered.

The coroner's inqueſt ſat upon the body, and brought in their verdict,

felo de ſe.

Canberra, 1st of October, 2016

For Sale: Number 453

I drive past the nondescript house,
remembering how ten years back
it was made infamous;
how I came to the roadblock
and matched it to the manhunt

unfolding in the news. I try to forget
the hogtied detail, the blunt
instruments of recall; take note
instead of that newly planted tree.

1768

I think of Laurence Sterne
on the anatomy table
the same year someone
collects Elizabeth Rainbow
from the foundling hospital.

Neither could know
of their multiple burials
or how many skulls or souls
might suffer the same fate.

The Pub with No Beer
(for FE)

Walking home past the village church, I'm drawn
to the lamplit window in the cottage
opposite, the old blacksmith's—before that
a pub: The New Slip Inn. (How come, this far
from a waterway?) The interior
is bedecked with memorabilia
that materialise, hammer and tongs
in the glow from a fire, wooden bellows
pumping the vision into life. Then it
cools, but somehow softens. It has the feel
of something dimly remembered, windows
opened in an old calendar. I lean
in to put right one of the slipped horseshoes
that has spilled its luck, making the world turn

upside down. I've passed through a cupboard door
and walked out onto a bleached veranda,
not that of my own childhood but one where
another family has assembled
for a shot outside The Pub with No Beer—
except the father has a glass of it.
He rests his forearms on the railing while
his son twists awkwardly bored, and mother
stands back in her sunnies. You, on the edge
of your new beauty, smile to camera,
a little white dog between your bare feet.
You're already telling me that the song's
what this is all about: Old Billy, a
blacksmith; how and when the warrigals called.

The Soldier's Tale
—*after Ramuz and Stravinsky, 1918*

Home had been in sight
but there were demons
still to battle—
and with little more
than your beloved fiddle,
pock-marked with shrapnel.
'Three days,' you vowed

> but three years
> you were away, in thrall
> to your troubles. It's dusk
> as you reapproach
> the outskirts of the village.
> You know the deal:
> step foot

across the border
and your secret kingdom's
null and void.
Instead, you send in a husk
of yourself to test the lie
of the familiar land—all
as you once knew:

       blacksmith's, school hall,
       church with steeple;
       coach-house weathervane
       swivelling on the roof;
       but here are the people,
       treating your survival
       with disdain,

seeing right through you
and your spoils of war;
your sweetheart
married, your mother deaf
to your ghostly sigh.
You poor, poor fool.
The devilish trickster

       is back at your shoulder
       mocking your desires:
       you thought you could add
       to the happiness you had
       but you can never share
       what you are
       with what you were.

In a Country Churchyard

It's late afternoon when I push the gate
and manoeuvre in the heavy mower.
Thirty years here, I'm still a newcomer
but there are names I recognise as well
as the next man: Foster, Duncan, Goodwill,
Robert and Molly Harding, and Lorna—
Lorna Lee, at whose grave my strong but frail
memory trembles, so that I lose all
grip and the engine cuts out... Her heart
had that same problem; for the infection
in her leg she suffered amputation
unanæsthetised. O what a feeble
thing, by comparison, at which to fail:
to mow the churchyard grass; or worse, to write.

Notes

Trench Cello
The 'Trench Cello' was made by W. E. Hill and Sons around 1900 as a portable 'holiday' instrument. Its owner, Harold Triggs, was a cello-playing insurance clerk sent to the front in 1915 with the Royal Sussex Regiment.

Fugue
Clement McWilliam was Sub-Organist, Winchester Cathedral, 1967-75.

A Night at the Opera
Martin Scorcese's film of Edith Wharton's novel, *The Age of Innocence* (1920), was released in 1993.

Rat Tales
The opening section is taken from *Straw Dogs* (dir. Sam Peckinpah, 1971); the closing section from *The Tale of Samuel Whiskers or The Roly-Poly Pudding*, by Beatrix Potter (Frederick Warne & Co., 1908).

A Speckled Hen
Rosalind Howard (1845–1921) became Countess of Carlisle and mistress of Castle Howard in 1888. She was president of the World Women's Temperance Association.

Brideshead Revisited
The Granada Television adaptation of Evelyn Waugh's 1945 novel was filmed at Castle Howard, North Yorkshire, and screened in 1980.

Miss Willmott's Ghost
Ellen Ann Willmott (1858–1934) was an English horticulturist who developed the gardens at Warley Place, Essex.

Page 147
'Paint her to your own mind' was an exhibition curated by the Laurence Sterne Trust at Shandy Hall in 2016. 147 writers and other artists interpreted the blank page that appears on page 147 of the original edition of *The Life and Opinions of Tristram Shandy, Gentleman*, Volume VI (1762).

Fire
Jonathan Martin (brother of the painter John Martin) set fire to York Minster on 1 February 1829.

Bring Me the Head, Camille
Sam Peckinpah's 1971 film, *Straw Dogs*, is based on *The Siege of Trencher's Farm*, a novel by Gordon Williams (1969). *Bring Me the Head of Alfredo Garcia* followed in 1974. Jerry Fielding wrote the scores for both—also for *The Wild Bunch*, nominated for an Oscar.

Macbeth
Kit Monkman's film adaptation of *Macbeth* is scheduled for release in 2017.

redruM, Steadicam, All Work and No Play
Stanley Kubrick's film, *The Shining*, based on Stephen King's novel, was released in 1980.

The Bulmer Murder
The italicised text is taken from *The Trial at Large of John Bolton, Gent.*, printed by N. Nickson in Blake Street, York.

1768
Laurence Sterne is believed to have been buried three times: twice at Hanover Square in London, 1768, and finally in Coxwold, 1969. Elizabeth Rainbow was one of many young people taken from Ackworth Hospital, West Yorkshire, (a branch of the Foundling Hospital in London) as 'apprentices'. Following abuse of this system, the hospital closed in 1773.

The Pub with No Beer
The beerless pub referenced is the Taylors Arm Hotel, NSW, where songwriter Gordon Parsons 'acquired' Dan Sheahan's 1943 poem based on the Day Dawn Hotel, QLD. Slim Dusty's 1957 recording made it famous. The New Slip Inn, Bulmer, was demolished and replaced by the blacksmith's shop in the early 1900s.

The Soldier's Tale
The text of Stravinsky's 1918 chamber work, *L'Histoire du Soldat*, was adapted by C. F. Ramuz from a Russian folk tale, 'The Runaway Soldier and the Devil'.

www.ingramcontent.com/pod-product-compliance
Lightning Source LLC
Chambersburg PA
CBHW032228080426
42735CB00008B/756